Making Wise

Investment Decision

Published by

Cryptocurrency World

COPYRIGHT

Contents

INTRODUCTION

Bitcoin, the world's most common and well known cryptocurrency, has been increasing in popularity. It has the same basic structure as it did when created in 2008, but repeat instances of the world market changing has created a new demand for cryptocurrencies much greater than its initial showing. By using a cryptocurrency, users are able to exchange value digitally without third party oversight. Cryptocurrency works on the theory of solving encryption algorithms to create unique hashes that are finite in number. Combined with a network of computers verifying transactions, users are able to exchange hashes as if exchanging physical currency. There is a finite number of bitcoin that will ever be generated, preventing an overabundance and ensuring its rarity. Water, despite its requirement as a life giving material, is generally accepted as being free or of little cost because it is so abundant. If water was rare, it would be more valuable than diamonds. Value exists for bitcoin because its users have trust that if they accept it as payment, they would could use it elsewhere to purchase something they want or need. As long as the users maintain this faith, the valued object can be anything. Bitcoin's value exists in its ecosystem much in the same way that wampum, a seashell, was the currency of the land for Native Americans. Bitcoin does not have intrinsic value like gold in that it cannot be used to make physical objects like jewelry that have value. Nevertheless, value continues to exist due to trust and acceptance.

Current legal and financial structures are not designed with a technology like this in mind. Financial institutions are built off of much older forms of currency. In some ways, it is comparative to the computing industry. The baseline of computing still relies on transmitting and processing 1's and 0's, providing only two dimensions of input. Yet all of our current technology uses this technologically archaic system due to adoption, cultivation, and lack of need for newer systems. If cryptocurrencies became the global norm for transactions, long standing systems for trade would need to be completely reformed to deal with this type of competition. For this reason, cryptocurrencies could possibly be the single most disruptive technology to global financial and economic systems.

Making Wise Investment Decision

BitPay, the largest bitcoin processor in the world, has recently seen transaction rate grow 110% in the past 12 months.

Transaction increase is an indicator of user acceptance growing. The conditions for Bitcoin's widespread adoption could be described as a "fire triangle". Where fire needs fuel, oxygen, and heat to exist; Bitcoin needs user acceptance, vendor acceptance, and innovation to ignite. Without all three aspects, bitcoin may not truly become a legitimized mainstream currency. Bitcoin is currently experiencing an increase in user acceptance and use, which is driving the other two aspects of the "fire triangle". Cryptocurrency's adoption will be an important subject to watch in the future, as it could be a truly transformative technology that alters the way money is exchanged worldwide. Bitcoin's increased adoption has been integrally tied to global market shifts. The current Internetfueled global market is very much entangled. If one regional market begins to plummet, it can easily drag the others with it. Bitcoin, like the Euro, can freely move across many national borders, creating an environment that promotes global trade, mutual prosperity, and even peace.

Cryptocurrency is the name given to a system that uses cryptography to allow the secure transfer and exchange of digital tokens in a distributed and decentralised manner.These tokens can be traded at market rates for fiat currencies. The first cryptocurrency was Bitcoin, which began trading in January 2009. Since then, many other cryptocurrencies have been created employing the same innovations that Bitcoin introduced, but changing some of the specific parameters of their governing algorithms. The two major innovations that Bitcoin introduced, and which made cryptocurrencies possible, were solutions to two long-standing problems in computer science: the double-spending problem and the Byzantine Generals Problem.

Double Spending

Until the invention of Bitcoin, it was impossible for two parties to transact electronically without employing a trusted third party intermediary. The reason was a conundrum known to computer scientists as the 'double spending problem', which has plagued attempts to create electronic cash since the dawn of the Internet.

Making Wise Investment Decision

To understand the problem, first consider how physical cash transactions work. The bearer of a physical currency note can hand it over to another person, who can then verify that he is the sole possessor of that note by simply looking at his hands. For example, if Alice hands Bob a

$100 bill, Bob now has it and Alice does not. Bob can easily verify his possession of the $100 bill and, implicitly, that Alice no longer has it. Physical cash transfers are also final, in the sense that to reverse a transaction the new bearer must give back the currency note. In our example, Bob would have to hand the $100 bill back to Alice. Given all of these properties, cash makes it possible for different parties, including strangers, to transact without trusting each other.

Now, consider how electronic cash might work. Obviously, paper notes would be out of the picture. There would have to be some kind of digital representation of currency. Essentially, instead of a $100 bill, we might imagine a $100 computer file. When Alice wants to send $100 to Bob, she attaches a $100 file to a message and sends it to him. The problem, as anyone who has sent an email attachment knows, is that sending a file does not delete it from one's com- puter. Alice will retain a perfect digital copy of the $100 she sends Bob, and this would allow her to spend the same $100 a second time, or indeed a third and fourth. Alice could promise to Bob that she will delete the file once he has a copy, but Bob has no way to verify this without trusting Alice.

Until recently, the only way to overcome the double spending problem was to employ a trusted third party intermediary. In our example, both Alice and Bob would have an account with a third party that they each trust, such as PayPal. Trusted intermediaries like PayPal keep a ledger of all account balances and transactions. When Alice wants to send $100 to Bob, she tells PayPal, which in turn deducts the amount from her account and adds it to Bob's. The transaction reconciles to zero. Alice cannot spend the same $100, and Bob relies on PayPal, which he trusts, to verify this. At the end of the day, all transfers among all accounts reconcile to zero. Note, however, that unlike cash, transactions that involve a third party intermediary are not final, as we have defined it, because transactions can be reversed by the third party.

In 2008, Satoshi Nakamoto (a pseudonym) announced a way to solve the double spending problem without employing third parties. His invention, Bitcoin, is essentially electronic cash. It allows for the first time the final transfer, not the mere copying, of digital assets in a way that can be verified by users without trusting other parties. This is accomplished through the clever use of public key cryptography, peer-to-peer networking and a proof-of-work system.

Like PayPal, the Bitcoin system employs a ledger, which is called the block chain. All trans- actions in the Bitcoin economy are recorded and reconciled in the block chain. However, unlike PayPal's ledger, the block chain is not maintained by a central authority. Instead, the block chain is a public document that is distributed in a peer-to-peer fashion across thousands of nodes in the Bitcoin network. New transactions are checked against the block chain to ensure that the same bitcoins have not been previously spent, but the work of verifying new transactions is not done by any one trusted third party. Instead, the work is distributed among thousands of users who contribute their computing capacity to reconcile and maintain the block chain ledger. In essence, the whole peer-to-peer network takes the place of the one trusted third party.

Byzantine Generals Problem

Bitcoin's solution to the double spending problem – distributing the ledger among the thousands of nodes in a peer-to-peer network – presents another problem. If every node on the network has a complete copy of the ledger that they share with the peers to which they connect, how does a new node connecting to the network know that she is not being given a falsified copy of the ledger? How does an existing node know that she is not getting falsified updates to the ledger? The difficult task of reaching consensus among distributed parties who do not trust each other is another longstanding problem in the computer science literature known as the Byzantine Generals Problem, which Bitcoin also elegantly solved.

The Byzantine Generals Problem posits that a number of generals each have their armies camped outside a city that they have surrounded. The generals know that their numbers are large enough that if half their combined force attacks at the same time they will take the city, but if they do not attack at the same time they will be spread too thinly and will be defeated. They can only communicate via messenger, and they have no way of verifying the authenticity of the messages being relayed. They also suspect that some of the generals in their ranks are traitors who will send fake messages along to their peers. How can this large group come to   a consensus on the time of attack without employing trust and without a central authority, especially when there will likely be attempts to confuse them with fake messages?

In essence, this is the same problem faced by Bitcoin's 'miners', the specialised nodes that verify new transactions and add them to the distributed ledger. Bitcoin's solution is to require additions to the ledger to be accompanied by the solution to a mathematical problem that is very difficult to solve but simple to verify. (This is much like calculating prime factors; costly   to do, but easy to check.) New transactions are broadcast in a peer-to-peer fashion across the network by parties to those transactions. Miners look at those transactions and confirm by checking their copy of the ledger (the block chain) that they are not double-spends. If they are legitimate transactions, miners add them to a queue of new transactions that they would like to add as a new page in the ledger (a new block in the block chain). While they are doing this, they are simultaneously trying to solve a mathematical problem in which all previous blocks in the block chain are an input. The miner that successfully solves the problem broadcasts his solution to the problem along with the new block to be added to the block chain. The other miners can easily verify whether the solution to the problem is correct, and if it is they add that new block to their copy of the block chain. The process begins anew with the new block chain as an input of the problem to be solved for the next block.

The mathematical problem in question takes an average of 10 minutes to solve. This is key because the important thing is not the solution itself, but that the solution proves that the miner has expended 10 minutes of work. On average, a new block is added to the block chain every 10 minutes because the problem that miners must solve takes on average 10 minutes to solve. However, if more miners join the network, or if computing power improves, the average time between blocks will decrease. To maintain the rate at which blocks are added to six per hour, the difficulty of the problem is adjusted every 2016 blocks (every two weeks). Again, the key here is to ensure that each block takes about 10 minutes to discover.

How does this solve the Byzantine Generals Problem? Suppose that a miner is confronted with two competing block chains (just as a general might receive messages with different attack times). To choose which chain to accept and work to extend, a miner can look to see which   is longer; that is, which chain has had the most processing power devoted to it. By always choosing the longest chain, an honest miner can ensure that he is in the company of at least 51% of the other honest miners. The gap between the longest chain and competing chains will grow as time passes, since the longer chain will have more processing power behind it.

New blocks contain not just the new transactions that have been broadcast on the network, but also a transaction that assigns the winning miner 25 newly created bitcoins, which incentivises them to dedicate their computing capacity to the network. The size of the reward to miners that accompanies new blocks also halves every 210,000 blocks (every four years). The reward began at 50 bitcoins with each block when the network was launched in 2009. Today the reward is 12.5 bitcoins and will halve again to 6.25 in 2020. This means that the total number of bitcoins that will ever exist will not exceed 21 million. As mining rewards diminish, what incentive will miners have to lend their computing power to verify transactions? The answer is that parties to a transaction can include a transaction fee to be paid to the miner who successfully adds their transaction to a block in the block chain.

THE ECONOMICS OF CRYPTOCURRENCY

Governance

Cryptocurrencies do not have central banks to regulate the money supply or oversee financial institutions, but no one should neglect the importance of cryptocurrency governance institutions. We focus our discussion on two separate but interrelated ways that cryptocurrencies can be said to be governed.

Algorithmic Governance

Rules for what are considered valid cryptocurrency transactions are embedded in the peer- to-peer software that cryptocurrency miners and users run. One valid kind of transaction is the creation of new coins out of thin air. Not everyone can execute this kind of transaction – miners compete for the right to execute one of these transactions per block (on Bitcoin, every ten minutes or so). When a miner discovers a valid hash for a block, they can claim the new coins.

A transaction in which a miner claims new coins, like any other transaction, has to conform to the expectations of the network. The network will reject a block that contains a transaction   in which a miner awards themselves too many new coins. The growth of coins is limited by a pre-determined amount per block.

On Bitcoin, the pre-determined amount is not scheduled to be constant over time, but rather is set to halve every 210,000 blocks, or about every four years, as described above. The total supply of bitcoins will asymptotically approach, but never exceed, 21 million. It will reach 20 million in 2025 and stop growing altogether in 2140.

Open Source Governance

The astute reader will note that the Bitcoin software that enforces particular rules about valid transactions and the rate of money creation does not appear out of thin air. Rather, the rules embedded in the software emerge from an interplay between leaders of the open source project that manages what is known as the 'reference client', other developers, miners, the user community and malicious actors. The dynamic between these players is as crucial to understanding Bitcoin as that of central banks, traditional monetary institutions and monetary politics is to understanding fiat currency.

Bitcoin, like all other even moderately successful cryptocurrencies to date, is a non-proprietary open source project. Users tend to look with suspicion on cryptocurrency projects that are closed source, that feature significant pre-mining in order to reward insiders, or that have other proprietary features. Other expectations of the user community also impose a check on developers. For example, the hard cap of 21 million bitcoins, while in principle subject to change through a software update, appears to   be non-negotiable for Bitcoin, although other cryptocurrencies have different money supply rules.

The division of Bitcoin software into a 'reference client' and so-called 'alt-clients' also has implications for Bitcoin's evolution. The community looks to the Bitcoin Core team for leadership as to the direction of the network. An alternative approach would be for the community to agree on the specification for the network, and then let independent teams write clients that implement the specification. The fact that Bitcoin has such a dominant reference client means that evolution can occur more quickly, although it may also have hidden costs. For example, the community has to put a lot of trust in the Bitcoin Core developers not to make bad changes to the network. A less concentrated approach to cryptocurrency development would slow down development, which would prevent any changes to the network without full deliberation of the community. It's possible that over time Bitcoin could move more to this model, but for now, the advantages of rapid evolution might outweigh the costs.

Miners also play an important role in governance. Because miners cryptographically guard against double spending, their consensus on what counts as a valid transaction is necessary for a cryptocurrency to function. A majority of miners must adopt any change to Bitcoin, and therefore the miners are able to impose a check on developers. Miners also exert influence through mining pools. Miners join pools in order to earn a more consistent payout. A single miner working alone might go for some time without discovering a block. But if miners pool their work and split their rewards, they can earn daily payouts.

Mining pools raise complications. For example, the biggest Bitcoin mining pool often has a third or more of the computing power of the Bitcoin network. If a pool ever obtained more than half of the network's computing power, it could double-spend. Double spending would destroy confidence in the Bitcoin network and would likely cause the price of bitcoins to plummet. Consequently, we observe some self-regulation by the mining pools, which are heavily invested in the success of Bitcoin. Whenever the top pool starts to approach 40% or so of computing power of the network, some participants exit the pool and join another one. So far this norm has persisted, but many in the community are concerned about mining pool concentration. Recently, the GHash.IO mining pool briefly exceeded 50 percent of Bitcoin's mining power. There is no evidence that the pool used its position to double spend, but many observers were alarmed that it was able to happen.

Concentrated mining pools have benefits as well as risks. In a crisis, it is useful to be able to assemble the key players. Such a crisis occurred on the night of 11 March 2013, when it became clear that a change in version 0.8 of the reference client introduced an unintentional incompatibility with version 0.7. As a result of the incompatibility, the two implementations of Bitcoin rejected each other's blocks, and the block chain 'forked' into two versions that did not agree on who owned which bitcoins. Within minutes of the realisation that there was a fork, the core developers gathered in a chat room and decided that the network should revert to the 0.7 rules. Over the next few hours, they were able to confer with the major mining pool operators and persuade them to switch back to 0.7, sometimes at a non-trivial cost to the miners who had mined coins on the 0.8 chain. The fact that mining pools are relatively concentrated meant that it was relatively easy to coordinate in the crisis. Within about seven hours, the 0.7 chain pulled permanently ahead and the crisis was resolved.

Another problem occurred in February 2014 when Mt. Gox, the oldest and largest Bitcoin exchange, claimedthatitsbitcoinholdingshadbeendepletedthrough'trans actionmalleability' attacks. Although it remains unclear whether Mt. Gox losses were really due to attacks, it became clear over the next several days that misunderstandings about transaction malleability were creating vulnerabilities. Some

Bitcoin sites temporarily suspended withdrawals while the issues were addressed by the core development team, which updated the Bitcoin software   and helped educate the community about transaction malleability, which, when properly understood, is a feature of Bitcoin, not a bug.

There is considerable scope for further study of cryptocurrency governance.

MEDIUM OF EXCHANGE VERSUS UNIT OF ACCOUNT

Bitcoin's lack of a central bank and fixed-trajectory money supply have earned it some criticism from economists concerned about macroeconomic stabilisation. Countercyclical inflationary stimulus is impossible.

However, this criticism may be misplaced. On most Keynesian and monetarist theories of monetary non-neutrality, the macroeconomic properties of money inhere in its unit-of- account function. Bitcoin is typically used as a medium of exchange without serving as a unit of account; that is, transactions will be denominated in dollars or another currency, but payment will be made using bitcoins. Unless prices, wages and contracts come to be denominated in Bitcoin, we would expect use of Bitcoin to have little cyclical impact.

Cryptocurrencies have a number of properties that make them especially useful as media of exchange, if not as units of account. Unlike paper money, they can be transacted online as well as in person, if an Internet connection is present. Unlike credit cards, the network fee for a simple cryptocurrency transaction is low and voluntary; it is used to incentivise rapid processing of transactions by the miners. Credit card networks typically charge a swipe fee   of 25b plus about 3% of the value of the transaction. On the Bitcoin network, transaction   fees are at most a few pennies. Some retailers use merchant services to accept Bitcoin- denominated payments and have the equivalent amount of dollars deposited directly in their bank accounts. The service providers commonly charge a 1% fee for this convenience, though this may decrease as hedging costs go down (discussed below). Even with this conversion   fee, merchants save 2% or more on transactions via the Bitcoin network. Another feature that could attract merchants is that customers who disavow a purchase cannot reverse most Bitcoin transactions, as they can credit card transactions.

In its separation of the medium of exchange and the unit of account, cryptocurrency brings   to life some creative research from the 1970s and 1980s by economists such as Fischer Black, Eugene Fama, Robert Hall and Neil Wallace. These authors regard the received monetary economics as highly contingent on legal and institutional arrangements; under laissez faire, they argue, we would observe explicit or implicit prices on media of exchange and a breakdown in the distinction between money and other financial assets. While cryptocurrency remains a niche payment mechanism and existing monetary institutions remain dominant, experimentation at the edges of our current monetary system with Bitcoin and other new cryptocurrencies could be fertile ground for new research in this tradition.

Pseudonymity and Censorship Resistance

Early news reports on Bitcoin focused on its use on the online black marketplace Silk Road. These reports propagated the misconception that Bitcoin transactions are anonymous. In fact, Bitcoin's ledger (called the block chain) is a completely public document. There is therefore a publicly accessible record of every Bitcoin transaction ever made. Bitcoin transactions occur between Bitcoin addresses, which are strings of random numbers and letters (a cryptographic hash of the address's public key). While there is no meaningful name attached to a transaction on the block chain, Bitcoin addresses function as pseudonyms for users. If a Bitcoin address can be identified as belonging to a particular individual, then all of the transactions on the block chain using that address can be attributed to that individual.

Users can take several steps to obfuscate identities and preserve some measure of financial privacy. They can generate and use a virtually unlimited number of addresses (there are 2160 valid Bitcoin addresses). It is considered best practice for merchants to generate a new receiving address for every transaction in order to protect their customers from scrutiny and to prevent espionage from competitors. It is also becoming increasingly common for transaction processors to collate several transactions into a single one so that no one knows which address is paying which. If Alice wishes to pay Bob and Charlie wishes to pay David, a single transaction in which Alice and Charlie put in money and Bob and David take it out can make it unclear who is paying whom.

Despite the availability of these steps, the Bitcoin network remains vulnerable to sophisticated analysis. Meiklejohn et al.were able to trace bitcoins from well-known thefts through the network to centralised services such as exchanges, which in principle could be subpoenaed to reveal the identities of the criminals. They used only publicly available data; a well-equipped law enforcement agency could de-anonymise the network even further.

Although transactions are not fully anonymous, Bitcoin represents a significant shift in the enforcement burden for illegal transactions. Because non-cryptocurrency electronic payments pass through financial intermediaries, governments can enforce restrictions on transactions by regulating those intermediaries. A drug dealer cannot generally accept Visa payments because Visa will not approve a merchant whose business is dealing drugs. Illegal Bitcoin transactions may be subject to ex post punishment, but they are not subject to prior restraint through the regulation of financial intermediaries. This could have a significant effect on the number and kind of laws that governments are able to economically enforce.

Future developments in cryptocurrency technology could bring strong anonymity to Bitcoin or another currency. Zerocash is one proposed anonymisation system that could either be added to a future iteration of Bitcoin or released as its own currency. The strong anonymity provided by Zerocash or a similar system could have significant implications for governments who rely on controlling the financial system to enforce laws.

Pricing and Volatility

Bitcoin traded over $1 for the first time in February 2011, for $30 in June 2011, below $7 in July 2011, below $2.50 in October 2011, climbed back up to $10 by August 2012, to over $230 in April 2013, fell to below $70 within a week and rose to over $1100 in November 2013 before falling by several hundred dollars again. This volatile trend raises questions about the price of cryptocurrencies: What is the fundamental value of a Bitcoin? Why is Bitcoin so volatile? What could increase or decrease the volatility of Bitcoin in the future?

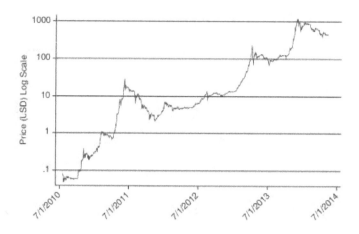

Since Bitcoin is not asset-backed, its value as a currency can only lie in its usefulness as a medium of exchange. As we have discussed, in some contexts, Bitcoin is superior to cash (e.g. it can be used online) and credit card payments (it is cheaper). In addition to its technical characteristics, its usefulness depends on the network effects that it can generate. The extent of future network effects remains uncertain, which is perhaps the biggest reason for the volatility of Bitcoin prices so far. Some of this uncertainty will necessarily resolve itself over time, as Bitcoin is revealed either to be valueless or to have enduring value. Bitcoin is always likely to be more volatile than fiat currencies, however, because it lacks a central bank and its supply is not responsive to changes in demand.

Cryptocurrencies also raise in a new way questions of exchange rate indeterminacy. As Kareken and Wallace observed, fiat currencies are all alike: slips of paper not redeemable for anything. Under a regime of floating exchange rates and no capital controls, and assuming some version of interest rate parity holds, there are an infinity of exchange rates between any two fiat currencies that constitute an equilibrium in their model.

The question of exchange rate indeterminacy is both more and less striking between cryptocurrencies than between fiat currencies. It is less striking because there are considerably more differences between cryptocurrencies than there are between paper money. Paper money is all basically the same. Cryptocurrencies sometimes have different characteristics from each other. For example, the algorithm used as the basis for mining makes a difference

–it determines how professionalised the mining pools become. Litecoin uses an algorithm that tends to make mining less concentrated. Another difference is the capability of the cryptocurrency's language for programming transactions. Ethereum is a new currency that boasts a much more robust language than Bitcoin. Zerocash is another currency that offers much stronger anonymity than Bitcoin. To the extent that cryptocurrencies differ from each other more than fiat currencies do, those differences might be able to pin down exchange rates in a model like Kareken and Wallace's.

On the other hand, exchange rate indeterminacy could be more severe among cryptocurrencies than between fiat currencies because it is easy to simply create an exact copy of an open source cryptocurrency. There are even websites on which you can create and download the software for your own cryptocurrency with a few clicks of a mouse. These currencies are exactly alike except for their names and other identifying information. Furthermore, unlike fiat currencies, they don't benefit from government acceptance or optimal currency area considerations that can tie a currency to a given territory.

Even identical currencies, however, can differ in terms of the quality of governance. Bitcoin currently has high quality governance institutions. The core developers are competent and conservative, and the mining and user communities are serious about making the currency work. An exact Bitcoin clone is likely to have a difficult time competing with Bitcoin unless it can promise similarly high-quality governance.

When a crisis hits, users of identical currencies are going to want to hold the one that is mostly likely to weather the storm. Consequently, between currencies with identical technical characteristics, we think governance creates something close to a winner-take-all market. Network externalities are very strong in payment systems, and the governance question with respect to cryptocurrencies in particular compounds them.

Cryptocurrency volatility could also be reduced by the introduction of exchange-traded futures and options markets. At present, the CFTC has still not opined on the legality of cryptocurrency derivatives. However, a number of Bitcoin-based businesses have been calling for the normalisation of hedging instruments for Bitcoin, which could also have the advantage of lowering merchant processing fees. Greater access to cryptocurrency derivatives is necessary for the health of the ecosystem. Some developers have begun work on decentralised derivatives exchanges, which could be important if financial regulators refuse to approve ordinary derivatives.

CONCLUSION

Cryptocurrency is an impressive technical achievement, but it remains a monetary experiment. Even if cryptocurrencies survive, they may not fully displace fiat currencies. As we have tried to show in this article, they provide an interesting new perspective from which to view economic questions surrounding currency governance, the characteristics of money, the political economy of financial intermediaries, and the nature of currency competition.

Cryptocurrency seems to have move past the early adoption phase that new technologies experience. Even motor vehicles experienced this phenomenon. Bitcoin has begun to carve itself a niche market, which could help advance cryptocurrencies further into becoming mainstream; or be the main cause of it failing. Cryptocurrencies are still in their infancy, and it is difficult to see if they will ever find true mainstream presence in world markets.

The Bitcoin community is striving to push into the mainstream through innovation and solving old problems.

Other forms of cryptocurrency have already emerged and have gained followings of their own, and each slightly different from Bitcoin and arguably as valid. Some nations like Iceland have even begun to start their own national cryptocurrencies. It possible that the future holds a place for cryptocurrency as a major currency solution, and Bitcoin will be instrumental in paving the way for those currencies to flourish. The European and Latin America markets are exploding with Bitcoin transactions, signifying true validity. Further topics to explore regarding Bitcoin and cryptocurrencies are quite numerous. Extensive studies should be performed on the economic effects of Bitcoin's effect on long standing fiat currency performance, and compare the results to countries that are beginning to adopt state-sponsored cryptocurrencies. The ability for cryptocurrency to perform micro transactions may allow it to bridge an economic gap that traditional state sponsored currencies would not be able to solve, but requires a much deeper market and economic analysis to determine. Also, the block chain technology that acts as Bitcoin's backbone has potential uses in other ways, such as smart contracts. These contracts are programmed payments that occur when a set condition occurs. Predetermined payment contracts are normally carried out by an entire accounting department of a company, making this an extremely interesting topic of further transformation. Lastly, cryptocurrency is a product of using cryptography to create a digital property. The frontier of digital property was popularized by the music industry"s shift to a cloud-based infrastructure. This frontier is still fairly new and unexplored, mainly populated by different types of media. Other forms of digital property may become as popular as music and cryptocurrency. Eight years ago, digital money was completely unheard of, and the creator of Bitcoin single handedly changed that. Cryptology, the root science beneath bitcoin and all cryptocurrencies, may be the mechanism behind the frontier for new and exciting digital inventions

DISCLAIMER

Disclaimer all the material contained in this book is provided for educational and informational purposes only. No responsibility can be taken for any results or outcomes resulting from the use of this material. While every attempt has been made to provide information that is both accurate and effective, the author does not assume any responsibility for the accuracy or use/ misuse of this information.

Notebook Space: _____

_____

_____

_____

_____

_____

_____

_____

_____

_____

_____

_____

_____

_____

_____

_____

_____

Making Wise Investment Decision